The
Huguenots
of *London*

For Jenny: may she find time to enjoy Huguenot London
as well as the delights of the modern city

The
Huguenots
of London

ROBIN GWYNN

THE ***A**lpha* PRESS

BRIGHTON • CHICAGO • TORONTO

First published in Great Britain in 1998, reprinted 2018, by
THE ALPHA PRESS
PO Box 139
Eastbourne BN24 9BP

Distributed in North America by
THE ALPHA PRESS
Independent Publishers Group
814 N. Franklin Street, Chicago, IL 60610

British Library Cataloguing in Publication Data
A CIP catalogue record for this book is available from the British Library.

Library of Congress Cataloging-in-Publication Data
Gwynn, Robin D.
The Huguenots of London / Robin Gwynn.
p.   cm.
Includes bibliographical references and index.
ISBN 9781898595243 (alk. paper)
1. Huguenots—England—London—History.
2. London (England)—Church history.
I. Title.
BX9458.G7G993 1998
284'.5'09421—dc21   98-15123

Typeset and designed by Sussex Academic Press, Brighton & Eastbourne.
Printed and bound by CPI Group (UK) Ltd, Croydon, CR0 4YY

Contents

List of Illustrations   vi

Acknowledgements   viii

England's Principal Refugee Centre   1

The French Church of London   9

The French Church of the Savoy   13

Contrasting Communities: Spitalfields and Soho   14

The Outlying Areas   22

London and Huguenot Settlement Elsewhere   24

Attitudes to the Refugees   27

The Huguenots and English Banking and Commerce   33

The Huguenots and Weaving   35

The Huguenots and other London Crafts and Professions   40

Assimilation   49

Appendix: A Visitor's Guide to Huguenot London   58

Select Bibliography   61

Index   64

List of Illustrations

Front cover: Silver watch by David Lestourgeon, 1702. Picture courtesy of the Museum of London, photographed by John Chase. *Back cover*: Silk design, dated May 12th, 1744, by Anna Maria Garthwaite (1690–1763). © Crown copyright, courtesy of The Victoria and Albert Museum.

1 Tympanum above doorway of the modern French Church of London.

2 Huguenots fleeing. Engraving by Jan Luyken, 1696.

3 The Dutch Church of Austin Friars. Courtesy of the Royal Commission on the Historical Monuments of England. © Crown Copyright.

4 French Church of London, Threadneedle Street. *The Graphic*, 24 October 1885. Private collection.

5 Sir Christopher Wren's design for enlarging the Savoy chapel, 1685. Courtesy of the Royal Collection.

6 Interior of l'Eglise des Grecs, Crown Street, Soho, 1819; watercolours by R. B. Schnebbelie. Photo courtesy of the Museum of London.

7 French churches in Spitalfields, 1700. Robin D. Gwynn, *Huguenot Heritage*, (Routledge & Kegan Paul, 1985), p. 102.

8 French churches in the western suburbs, 1700. Robin D. Gwynn, *Huguenot Heritage* (Routledge & Kegan Paul, 1985), p. 104.

9 and 10 The former French church at Fournier Street/Brick Lane, Spitalfields. Courtesy of Tower Hamlets Education & Community Services – Local History Library & Archives.

11 The Spitalfields area, from John Rocque's Plan of the Cities of London and Westminster (1746). Courtesy of the Keeper of Prints and Maps, Corporation of London. Photo: Godfrey New Photographics.

12 Borough of Wandsworth, Armorial Bearings.

13 The *London Gazette* reports attacks on Protestantism in France, 1682.

14 Hogarth's *Noon*. Engraving, first state, 1738. Photo, courtesy of the Museum of London.

15 Bank note from Minet and Fector's, 1797. Courtesy of The Huguenot Library, University College, London WC1E 6BT.

16 Crystal glass from Verzelini's London glasshouse, 1581. Courtesy of the Victoria and Albert Museum.

17 John de Planche, binding of Gospels in Anglo-Saxon, 1571. Courtesy of the British Library.

18 State Coach of the Speaker of the House of Commons, designed by

Daniel Marot, 1698. Engraving, *Illustrated London News*, 1847. Courtesy of the Mary Evans Picture Library.

19 Wrought-iron balustrade, probably by Jean Tijou. Courtesy of the Victoria and Albert Museum.

20 Pair of flintlock holster pistols by Pierre Monlong, *c.* 1695.

21 Silver-gilt ewer by Pierre Harache the younger, 1705–6. Courtesy of the Vintners' Company of London.

22 Abraham de la Neuvemaison becomes Abraham Newhouse; four successive annual receipts, 1776–79. Courtesy of The Huguenot Library.

23 1803 Declaration of London merchants.

24 French Hospital, near Old Street.

25 Seal of *La Providence.*

26 Receipt issued by the Westminster French Protestant School, 1791. Courtesy of The Huguenot Library, University College, London WC1E 6BT.

27 French Church of London, Soho Square; engraving, 1893. Photo, courtesy of the Museum of London.

The author and publisher gratefully acknowledge permission to reproduce the illustrations detailed above. The publisher apologizes for any errors or omissions in the above list, and would be grateful to be notified of any corrections that should be incorporated in the next edition or reprint of this book.

Acknowledgements

The inspiration for this book arose out of discussions with Valerie Cumming, Tessa Murdoch and Rosemary Weinstein at the Museum of London at the time of its *Quiet Conquest* exhibition in 1985, and the Museum has been consistently encouraging and helpful since. I particularly appreciate its generosity in providing and authorising the use of a number of the illustrations reproduced here.

I also acknowledge with grateful thanks the support and assistance of the late Irene Scouloudi and of Randolph Vigne, successive editors of the *Proceedings* of the Huguenot Society of Great Britain and Ireland, and the contribution made to our knowledge of the subject by so many scholars in the pages of the Society's publications. Yves Jaulmes and the Consistory of the French Church of London have also been unfailingly helpful.

Much of the appendix, a visitor's guide to Huguenot London today, is based on a leaflet I wrote for the "Huguenot Heritage" tercentenary which was published in 1985 by the English Tourist Board in association with the Huguenot Society.

Robin Gwynn

The Huguenots of London

England's Principal Refugee Centre

The population of London (taking the area in which bills of mortality were collected to warn of the onset of plague) was perhaps 50,000 in 1500, 200,000 by 1600, half a million by 1700, 675,000 by 1750.[1] There were always more deaths than births in early modern London, so its remarkable growth between the sixteenth and eighteenth centuries depended chiefly on immigration from the provinces. The capital attracted English men and women from throughout the country even though, with its immorality and criminal underworld, it also disgusted them. It was, after all, the seat of the royal court and of Parliament and of the law courts; and it combined the role of capital city with that of great port. It was the one great English financial centre, the hub of overseas trade, the deep-water shipping centre, connected by invisible but powerful links to all major provincial towns and to the other great cities of Europe.

By 1700 it was over twenty times the size of the next largest English city, and one in every nine or ten Englishmen was a Londoner. It was the centre of fashion, of specialised crafts and skills, of theatre and of every kind of entertainment from the lewd to the sophisticated. It had an amazing number of alehouses and inns, coffee houses, eating places. It was a manufacturing centre, and the national centre for the distribution of goods of all sorts.

Here then was a dynamically expanding city where fortunes might be made, powerful connections could be developed,

---

[1] Roger Finlay, *Population and Metropolis: the demography of London 1580–1650* (Cambridge, 1981), p. 51, with the figure for 1700 reduced towards his later estimate in the opening chapter of A. L. Beier and Roger Finlay (eds), *London 1500–1700* (London, 1986).

employment might be found; a place where native ingenuity and hard work could hope to be rewarded. If newcomers approached it with such optimistic thoughts, the great majority were doomed to bitter disappointment. The story of Dick Whittington dates from the late sixteenth century, but for most arrivals the sad reality was not a future paved with gold but a tenuous, shabby, under-employed existence in overcrowded and unhygienic tenements. Still, London offered at least a glimmer of hope to men and women short of choices. And for the same reasons as it drew people from all over England, the capital acted as a magnet to people displaced from other European countries, so that when an observer writing in 1751 maintained that immigrants from overseas "have been wholly possessed by London",[2] there was some truth behind his exaggeration.

In addition to the potential openings it offered, London was the only place in England where "strangers", the contemporary term for what we would now call foreigners, had the possibility of dis-appearing into an anonymous mass while they tried to come to terms with English ways and language. It was also the centre where they were most likely to find fellow-countrymen to lessen their feelings of insecurity and give them support as they made the difficult transition in their lives. A foreigner was less of a stranger in such a metropolis.

Foreigners of all sorts have had a major role to play throughout London's history. Long before the Reformation, there had been Jews (until their expulsion in 1290) and Lombards, Dutchmen and the German merchants from the Hanseatic League who, operating from their headquarters at the Steelyard in Thames Street, main-tained a privileged position in London's trade until the mid-Tudor

---

[2] Quoted in Daniel Statt, *Foreigners and Englishmen: the controversy over immigration and popula-tion, 1660–1760* (Newark, 1995), p. 31.

period. In recent times we have seen refugees from Hitler's Germany, and waves of West Indian and Asian immigrants. This short book focusses on one particular group of overseas immigrants, the Huguenots, French-speaking Protestants. Those who came to England were for the most part taking refuge from religious disturbances on the mainland of Europe in the sixteenth and early seventeenth centuries, and from persecution in France in the late seventeenth and eighteenth centuries.

Both key words in the title are capable of a number of definitions. "London" could be taken as the city within the walls, or the area of municipal jurisdiction which extended without the walls and encompassed Southwark, or the city of London together with the neighbouring city of Westminster (from which in 1500 it was still separated by a green belt). Here the widest possible definition has been used; French Protestant communities have been considered within the whole area of modern Greater London, including those some miles away from the city at Greenwich and Wandsworth.

"Huguenots" can also be taken narrowly or broadly: narrowly, as Calvinists from France; broadly, as Protestants who spoke a French-based language, which definition includes some Swiss, Protestants from the principality of Orange, and most importantly Walloons from the area of the southern Netherlands. The Walloon refugees of Queen Elizabeth I's reign came from the dominions of the Spanish king Philip II (then the ruler of what is modern Belgium), rather than those of the King of France. In practice, it is virtually impossible for the historian of French Protestants in sixteenth-century England to separate Walloons from French, since they worshipped together in the same congregations and were lumped together in English understanding simply as "French". Within the congregations themselves, it was another matter. There the distinction was well understood, and the minister of the French

Church of London reported in 1591 that "one part, and that the least" of his congregation in Threadneedle Street "were Frenchmen ... the other part, and that the greatest, were ... sprung out of the countries which obey the Spaniard; and in less need and want (some few excepted) than the rest".[3] While sixteenth century French-speaking refugees might be either Huguenot or Walloon, their successors in the seventeenth and eighteenth centuries were almost all French Calvinists, and it is on these that this book principally concentrates.

With the notable exception of Andrew Pettegree's *Foreign Protestant Communities in Sixteenth-Century London*,[4] which concentrates on the early period from the 1540s to the 1570s, there is a lack of substantial books on the Huguenots in the English capital. Considering that there were between 20,000 and 25,000 French Protestant refugees crowded into the eastern and western suburbs by the close of the seventeenth century[5], the lack is surprising: all the more so since lengthy accounts do exist of the history of the smaller French-speaking communities of Canterbury and Norwich[6], and much work has been done on the Dutch in London.[7] King Edward VI granted a charter establishing foreign Protestant churches in the capital in 1550 (Plate 1). From then until the eventual assimilation of the Huguenots into English society, accomplished by the end of the eighteenth century, London remains the key to any full understanding both of Huguenot settle-

---

[3] J. Strype, *Annals of the Reformation* (4 vols, Oxford, 1824), IV, pp. 114–15.
[4] Published by the Clarendon Press, Oxford, 1986.
[5] Robin Gwynn, "The Number of Huguenot Immigrants in England in the Late Seventeenth Century", *Journal of Historical Geography*, vol. 9, no. 4 (1983): 391–3.
[6] In volumes 1 and 15 of the Quarto Series Publications of the Huguenot Society of Great Britain and Ireland.
[7] J. H. Hessels (ed.), *Ecclesiae Londino-Batavae Archivum* (3 vols, the third in two parts, Cambridge, 1887–97); J. Lindeboom, *Austin Friars: history of the Dutch Reformed Church in London 1550–1950* (The Hague, 1950); David Ormrod, *The Dutch in London: the influence of an immigrant community 1550–1800* (HMSO for the London Museum, 1973); Ole Peter Grell, *Dutch Calvinists in Early Stuart London: the Dutch church in Austin Friars 1603–1642* (Leiden, 1989).

PLATE 1: *Tympanum above the doorway of the French Church of London in Soho Square today, commissioned in 1950 to mark the fourth centenary of the church. The sculptor was J. Prangnell. Although the letters patent founding the church in 1550 were made out to "Germans and other foreigners", the churches founded as a result were Dutch and French.*

ment patterns in the country as a whole, and of what the refugees gave to Britain.

It seems to have been the very size of the French community in and around London that has deterred historians, coupled with the amazing number of congregations it spawned around 1700 and the scattered and erratic nature of the available evidence. Some gaps in our knowledge will never be filled, but it is far more complete than formerly it was. A glance at the Bibliography will confirm that there is no longer any excuse for the ignorance that once enabled an official Home Office Report to talk of 26 French churches in the London region at a time when there was actually only one.[8] Nor should it be possible for historians to make the reverse

---

[8] *Report with Evidence and Appendices of the Committee appointed by the Secretary of State for the Home Department to inquire as to the History and Constitution of the French Protestant Church of London* (1913), p. 5.

PLATE 2:   *Huguenots fleeing. Engraving by Jan Luyken, 1696.*

"[During the persecution of 1686] Elizabeth and her husband and child were obliged to refuge in woods near Boulogne for several days and nights, during which time they were robbed of what they had and at last obliged to go home again... At his coming back [the husband] was apprehended and put in prison, during which time she was brought to bed of her daughter Mary and by intercession of friend he was some time after released out of prison, and in order to their more easily making their escape, they went to live at Marcq near Calais, and by God's grace and my providing a boat to come on the French shore from Dover, etc both her said husband, herself, 2 children and his mother came in the night in a wagon that I had also provided from Marcq to the sea shore off of petite wall, and on the first August 1686 landed at Dover."

Isaac Minet (1660–1745) describes the escape of his sister Elizabeth in his "Relation of our Familly"; *Proceedings of the Huguenot Society*, II (1887–88), 432–3 [spelling modernised].

error, as has also sometimes been done, and assume that all mentions of a French congregation must refer to one and the same church.

Focus on the congregations is inevitable, for the Huguenots in exile – especially those who came in the decade of greatest immigration, the 1680s – were not forced out of their home country but became refugees voluntarily for the sake of their religion. At that time 200,000 or a quarter of a million of them settled in England, the Netherlands, other parts of Europe, America and the Cape of Good Hope because of religious persecution. From 1681 they were subject to the *dragonnades*, an effective method of forced "conversion", and in 1685 the Revocation of the Edict of Nantes withdrew all recognition of Protestantism in France. Since emigration was strictly prohibited, the immigrants who came to England had run a gauntlet through patrolling soldiers or guardships to make good their escape (Plate 2). Most had made substantial material sacrifices for the sake of their beliefs. Naturally, therefore, they wanted to worship in the company of their countrymen and co-religionists, so initially it is through their congregations that historians can best hope to trace their presence in England.

When the main bulk of refugees arrived, there were already two well-established French churches in the London area: one at Threadneedle Street in the City, which continued to go by the name of the "French Church of London" long after many others had been established; the other at the Savoy in Westminster. New immigrants tended to be drawn to one or the other. The two were strikingly different in their organization, mode of worship, history and connections, and it is partly in reflection of these differences that the French communities of east and west London evolved in distinctive ways.

The French Church of London

The French Church of London already had a long and distinguished history by the time the actions of King Louis XIV of France caused some forty or fifty thousand new migrants to cross the Channel. It shared a charter, and once a month exchanged church buildings, with the Dutch Church of Austin Friars, also founded in 1550. These foreign churches may have been established "as much more than a home from home for foreign Protestant refugees",[9] indeed as a model for what the Church of England was to become. That was not to be, for Edward VI's sisters, first the strongly Roman Catholic Mary and then the conservative though Protestant Elizabeth, did not share their brother's advanced Reformed views. However the congregations, in any case, tended to view themselves as candles to the world during the first century of their existence, and to pride themselves on the purity of their Protestant doctrine and organization. "Observe their order, their unity, their wise discipline", it was remarked of the leaders of the French church of London in the early Stuart period, "and you will say that God dwells in their midst".[10] Strategically placed in the capital of one of the most powerful Protestant kingdoms in Europe, the churches were considered by European Calvinist leaders to be of more than ordinary importance, and John Calvin himself released one of his most trusted lieutenants, Nicolas des Gallars, to serve the French Church of London.

The Threadneedle Street church, then, was already well-known

---

[9] Patrick Collinson, "England and International Calvinism 1558–1640", in Menna Prestwich (ed.), *International Calvinism 1541–1715* (Oxford, 1985), p. 199.
[10] A. de Rocquigny, *La Muse Chrestienne* (1634), p. 8.

PLATE 3:   The Dutch Church of London at Austin Friars. The French and Dutch
church buildings were exchanged by their congregations one Sunday a month until
1799, when the exchange was limited to once a year.

on the Continent at the time when the fate of the Huguenots was
being settled during the reign of Louis XIV in France (1660–1714).
It was by far the biggest French congregation in England. It was
also well organised and very active. Its vitality was clearly shown
in the way it cared for its sick members during the Great Plague of
1665, and by the remarkable speed with which its Consistory, or
governing body, caused the church to be rebuilt after it was totally
destroyed during the disaster of the Fire of London the following
year (Plate 4); the new building reopened in the summer of 1669,
whereas the general rebuilding of local English parish churches
only got under way in the 1670s. Worship at Threadneedle Street
followed the familiar forms beloved by French Protestants; and the

PLATE 4:   *French Church of London, Threadneedle Street.*

legality of its existence was unquestionable – no small matter in the years after the Restoration, when the ruling Establishment in England was persecuting English Dissenters, some of whose beliefs and practices were similar to those of the refugees.

On the other hand, against these positive recommendations had to be set the strained relations that existed between the Threadneedle Street congregation and the royal court. During the Civil War, most church members had been strongly Parliamentarian, and one minister, Jean de la Marche, had called for the execution of King Charles I as early as November 1645. His royalist colleague and rival, Louis Hérault, had been driven out two years earlier. After the Restoration of the monarchy in 1660, Charles II ordered that Hérault should be recalled, but the pastor continued to be thoroughly unpopular. In 1676 Hérault was forced to retire once again, but not before he had written repeatedly to influential ministers of state describing the elders of the church in terms that questioned their loyalty to the throne.[11] Then came the Exclusion Crisis of 1679–81, and once more the principal members of the Threadneedle Street church crossed the wishes of England's rulers; indeed the two Whig sheriffs of London elected in 1682 in opposition to the Court's preferred candidates were Thomas Papillon and John Dubois, both of Huguenot descent and both past members of the Consistory of the Threadneedle Street church. The Court had already sent a sharp reminder to the church that it existed only by royal favour. Since the *dragonnades* had started in France in 1681, the timing could hardly have been worse from the point of view of Huguenots newly crossing the Channel, and the warm welcome they received from Charles II is all the more remarkable.

---

[11] For instance, Public Record Office, SP/29/382, no. 195.

The French Church of the Savoy

The French church of the Savoy had a strikingly different past. It was much younger, finding its origins in the preaching of Jean d'Espagne to the west of London on the eve of the Civil War. A man of more moderate temper than either De la Marche or Hérault, d'Espagne drew about him a congregation which can be best described as moderate Parliamentarian, but which was well-connected with a number of gentry and included known royalists like the mathematician Isaac de Caus and the coin-engraver Nicholas Briot. The Threadneedle Street church claimed the right to supervise all French Protestants in the London area, and repeatedly attempted to bring the Westminster group into its orbit. After the Restoration, Charles II was confronted by two petitions: one from the City church which had just recalled Hérault, asking for an end to the existence of its western rival; the other from the Westminster church, stressing its loyalty to the Crown and requesting independent authorization.

The solution adopted in 1661 was novel and important. The existing Westminster congregation was prohibited, but at the same time offered a new lease of life – and granted the use of the Savoy Chapel – provided it conformed to the Church of England. Worship at the Savoy, therefore, did not follow the lines to which the new Huguenot refugees were accustomed. Rather, it used the Anglican prayer book translated into French, which lacked appeal to many of those taking refuge to worship in the way they believed fitting. On the other hand, the Westminster church had close and valuable connections with influential people at Court and in the Church of England.

Contrasting Communities: Spitalfields and Soho

Not only were the French churches of Threadneedle Street and the Savoy divided by character, history, and type of worship, but the members of the congregations to the east and west of London pursued quite different trades. To the east, a very large proportion of the artisans who composed the bulk of the congregations in the Spitalfields area were associated with the weaving trade, and there were large numbers of ministers and a significant number of naval personnel. In the western suburbs, by contrast, weavers were few, but there were far more soldiers (many of them officers), intellectuals, and tradesmen involved in fashionable trades: hairdressers, jewellers, shoemakers, silversmiths, tailors, watchmakers, wigmakers and the like. Since it was very often employment opportunities that determined where new refugees eventually settled, this difference was highly significant.

Nearly half a century ago, E. H. Varley extracted figures from some published Huguenot church registers which happened to include specific entries giving trades. The total numbers are not significant, since it was mere chance or the efficiency of individual clerks that caused the trades to be recorded in some cases but not others. Nevertheless, the entries offer a valuable snapshot of the startling differences in the composition of the settlements to the east and west of the capital. Reworking Varley's figures,[12] which relate to the period 1689–1716, one finds:

---

[12] "The Occupations of Protestant Refugees in the Seventeenth Century", *Geography*, XXIV (1939): 133.

	Eastern London	Western London
Doctors and Ministers	160	86
Food, drink and clothing	24	207
Jewellers, Clockmakers etc	8	119
Merchants	31	100
Military	4	131
Naval	60	11
Perruquiers	8	53
Textile workers	465	44
All others	81	330

As Huguenots streamed into London in the 1680s, the Threadneedle Street and Savoy churches consolidated and further defined their areas of special influence. Their buildings could not cope with the new crowds (Plate 5), and economic reasons encouraged recent arrivals to cluster some distance away from them, in the suburbs. The Threadneedle Street church established a large annexe to the east, "L'Eglise de l'Hôpital", in Spitalfields; the Savoy opened one to the west, "L'Eglise des Grecs", in Soho (Plate 6). Still refugees poured in, and more French churches were necessary. By 1690 there were three or four in the eastern suburbs, ten in the western. Ten years later there were nine in the east, all worshipping in the traditional way of the French Church of London; and fourteen in the west, equally divided between the old French and the Savoy's new Anglican pattern of worship (Plates 7 and 8).

Of these two communities, the one in the east was clearly the larger and more homogeneous. There were so many weavers in the eastern suburbs that the Weavers' Company found it desirable to appoint a French-speaking clerk, and Londoners complained that it was difficult to hear English spoken in some of the streets of Spitalfields. United to a large extent by trade as well as by

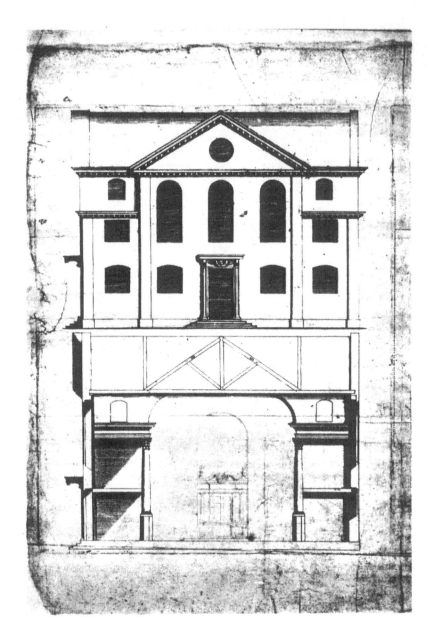

PLATE 5:   *Sir Christopher Wren's design for enlarging the Savoy chapel, it being now "much too little for the congregacon", 1685.*

PLATE 6: *Interior of l'Eglise des Grecs, Crown Street, Soho, 1819; watercolours by R. B. Schnebbelie. This church, which got its name because it had originally been built for a Greek Orthodox congregation, became the foremost conformist church in London (and England) after the closure of the Savoy chapel in the 1730s.*

language and religion, the refugees in the Spitalfields area formed a ghetto more resistant to assimilation than their settlement in the Soho region. In the western suburbs, with trades involving more direct contact with English customers and often with an Anglican form of religion, assimilation was somewhat quicker. Even so, over half a century after the Revocation Lord Chesterfield was advising Englishmen who might be contemplating a visit to France to further their education to go to Westminster instead, and Hogarth's *Noon* (Plate 14) likewise shows the French community remaining distinctive. Street names remain in both Soho (Foubert's Place, Romilly Street) and Spitalfields (Fournier Street, Leman Street) to recall their Huguenot past.

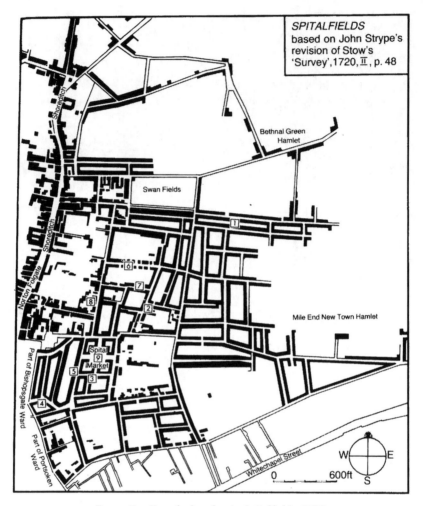

SPITALFIELDS
based on John Strype's
revision of Stow's
'Survey',1720, Ⅱ, p. 48

Bethnal Green
Hamlet

Swan Fields

Mile End New Town Hamlet

Part of Bishopsgate Ward

Part of Portsoken Ward

Spital
Market

Norton Folgate

Shoreditch

Whitechapel Street

0   600ft

PLATE 7:   *French churches in Spitalfields, 1700.*

Prominent in modern Spitalfields, on the corner of Fournier
Street and Brick Lane, stands a building which sums up much of
the area's history in an extraordinary way (Plates 9 and 10). Today
it is a mosque; previously it was the Great Synagogue for the
Ashkenazi Jews; before that, a Methodist chapel; and in origin, a
Huguenot church, the successor to l'Eglise de l'Hôpital. It was
built in 1742–4, at a time when a number of other French congrega-

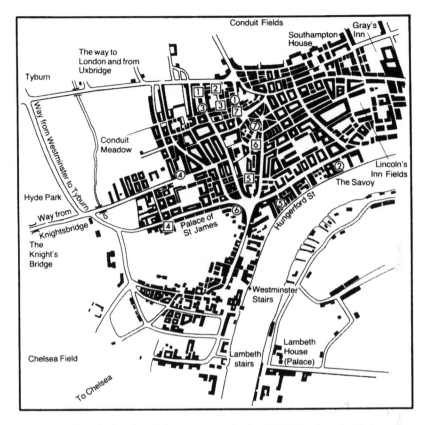

PLATE 8: *French churches in the western suburbs, 1700. Numbers in circles represent churches worshipping along the lines of the French church of the Savoy, those in squares represent churches worshipping in the traditional Huguenot way.*

tions already existed in the region, and its size emphasizes how large, how concentrated, and how devoted to its beliefs the east London Huguenot community remained even two generations after the Revocation of the Edict of Nantes. The fact that the vaults under the church were always intended to be let to brewers and vintners as cellars for the storage of beer and wine also testifies to the canny business sense of the Huguenots.

Plates 9 and 10: Two photographs of the former French church at the corner of Fournier Street and Brick Lane, Spitalfields. At the time the photographs were taken, the building was a synagogue; it is now a mosque. The date 1743 is above the sundial.

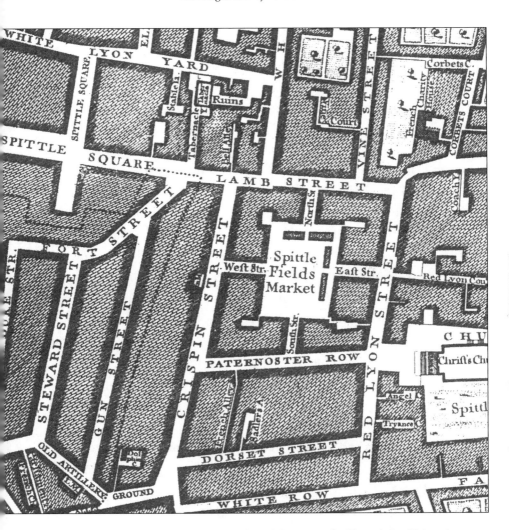

Plate 11: Part of the Spitalfields area, from John Rocque's Plan of the Cities of London and Westminster and Borough of Southwark, published in 1746 in 24 sheets. John Rocque, engraver, surveyor and mapmaker, was himself of Huguenot descent. This section of the map around Spitalfields Market includes French Alley between Paternoster Row and Dorset Street, the French Charity House near Corbets Court (top right), and the French Church of the Artillery (bottom left). Three other French congregations had been meeting in this small area at the start of the century.

The Outlying Areas

While by far the greatest concentrations of Huguenots were cen-
tred on Spitalfields and Soho, other communities developed in the
outskirts beyond the London-Westminster conurbation. The areas
in question have since been swallowed up by the continuing
growth of the capital, but at the close of the seventeenth century
they were in the country and shared the advantages enjoyed by the
extremities of the built-up region – in particular, cheaper housing.
French schools run by refugees opened at such places as Islington
and Marylebone, and at Chelsea, where Huguenot gardeners also
settled. The community at Hoxton was big enough to maintain a
French church until 1785. Sunbury-on-Thames became the location
of a colony of Huguenot gentlefolk who also had residences in
Westminster, while a French church composed primarily of the
families of seamen from the Channel Islands developed at
Wapping.

The earliest and most interesting of these outlying Huguenot settlements – both formed in the 1680s, but as different from one
another as those of Spitalfields and Soho – were at Greenwich and
Wandsworth. The diarist John Evelyn recorded attending the
French service at Greenwich in 1687, finding the preacher "patheti-
caly perswading to patience, constancy and relyance on God, for
the comfort of his Grace, amidst all their Sufferings".[13] There were
Huguenot glassmakers at Greenwich, but what remain to catch the
eye today are the fine houses of Crooms Hill where, in the eighteenth century, there lived members of the families of Breholt,

---

[13] E. S. de Beer (ed.), *The Diary of John Evelyn* (6 vols, Oxford, 1955), IV, p. 548.

Delamotte, Ducarrel, Girardot, Guigier, Lapostre, Layard, Nogee, Olivier, Remy, Savary and Teulon.

Wandsworth's French residents, of whom there were hundreds, tended to be of a lower social class. They included numerous felt-makers, hatmakers and dyers who had moved away from London primarily to escape guild restrictions. Apparently they were successful in this, for in 1694 the Feltmakers Company of London decided to allow any lawful feltmaker to employ provincial journeymen in manufacturing hats of French design in Wandsworth, Battersea and Lambeth "so that all theire Majesties Subjects and Freemen of London might have the same privileges that the French and foreigners had".[14] In any event the Huguenot hatmakers found the river Wandle well suited to their needs, and a pleasing story tells how cardinals from Rome were forced to send to Wandsworth for their red hats. The borough bears reminders of its Huguenot past in its coat-of-arms (Plate 12) and in the nearest approach in England to a Huguenot cemetery, the graveyard long popularly called "Mount Nod".

---

[14] Norman G. Brett-James, *The Growth of Stuart London* (London, 1935), p. 492.

London and Huguenot Settlement Elsewhere

By 1700, at least half the refugees from Louis XIV's reign who crossed the Channel were living in what is now the region of Greater London, drawn there by employment opportunities, friends or contacts, and the need for advice and companionship. Others were spread throughout south-western and south-eastern England, but all were influenced by decisions made in the capital, for London was the centre of the massive efforts undertaken from the 1680s onwards to relieve the poor and support the ministry of the word among the many French congregations. One of the features that distinguished England from other places of Huguenot refuge was that relief was organised in a highly centralised manner, and publicly sponsored; and London was the organisational hub.

Some communities had even more direct links. The small group at Southampton could hardly have survived the middle decades of the seventeenth century without financial help from the capital. It was from London that the influence of the Threadneedle Street church and Bishop Compton combined to ensure a settlement of Huguenot fishermen at Rye in 1681. The same powerful combination, with the assistance of the philanthropist Thomas Firmin, also undertook a more ambitious venture involving linen- and silk-weavers at Ipswich. The Threadneedle Street church even concerned itself with settlements across the Atlantic in St Christopher (West Indies) and Carolina, Pennsylvania and Boston.[15]

---

[15] French Church of London Library, MS 5, pp. 682, 692; Huguenot Society of Great Britain and Ireland Quarto Series, vol. LVIII (1994): 143, 312.

PLATE 12: *Wandsworth's armorial bearings. Teardrops on gold squares represent the sufferings of the Huguenots.*

The importance of London can also be gauged from the best-known contemporary Huguenot memoirs, those of Jaques Fontaine. While he himself took refuge in Devon and moved from there to Somerset and then Ireland, the English capital was critical to the fortunes of his family from Saintonge. Of his ten brothers and sisters, half-brothers and half-sisters, five had close connections with London. His eldest half-sister Jane died there, and three of her five children went there too. The next half-sister Judith like-wise sought refuge in London with her eldest daughter, where they were joined by her second daughter. One half-brother, Pierre, settled in London with his family, as did the widow of another. His full sister Marie and her husband ended up in Balk in Friesland but did so via the English capital, and four of their children settled in London. As for Jaques himself, when in 1694 he was moving from Taunton to Ireland and wanted to send his eldest sons James and Aaron to Amsterdam, it was to London that he took them. Later his son Peter was to leave for Virginia via London, and another son John established himself in the capital as a watch and clockmaker.[16] Many other Huguenot families had multiple connections with London in this kind of way.

---

[16] Dianne W. Ressinger (ed.), *Memoirs of the Reverend Jaques Fontaine 1658–1728* (Huguenot Society New Series No. 2, London, 1992), pp. 43–4, 46–7, 56, 147, 191, 219, 230.

Attitudes to the Refugees

Not all Englishmen took the same positive approach towards the refugees as Bishop Compton and Thomas Firmin. Londoners had a long history of antagonism towards foreigners present in their midst; indeed during the Middle Ages their feelings had sometimes been vented in massacre, as in 1189–90, when Jews were the victims, or 1381, when Flemings were one of the targets during the Peasants' Revolt. After the "evil May Day" riot aimed against foreigners in 1517, fifteen Londoners were hung, drawn and quartered. Such strong feeling could hardly be expected simply to dissipate in the face of so many new arrivals in the Elizabethan and Stuart periods, and it certainly did not do so. In 1593 an attack on the London immigrant community was mooted, and a verse appeared pinned to the door of the Dutch Church of London:

> You strangers that inhabit this land!
> Note this same writing, do it understand;
> Conceive it well, for safety of your lives,
> Your goods, your children, and your dearest wives.

An eighteenth-century French visitor, J. P. Grosley, described how "at the corner of every street" he was met by

> a volley of abusive litanies, in the midst of which I slipt on, returning thanks to God that I did not understand English. The constant burthen of these litanies was, French dog, French b——; to make any answer to them was accepting a

challenge to fight; and my curiosity did not carry me so far.[17]

By the time of the Restoration, in many English minds the French were once more the national enemies they had always traditionally been in the late Middle Ages, before Philip II and the Armada had made the Spanish threat loom closer. "We do naturally all love the Spanish and hate the French", Samuel Pepys recorded in his Diary in 1661. The mistaken belief that foreigners were responsible for deliberately starting the Great Fire was widespread, and added an element of fear and panic to the xenophobia that already existed. More rationally, it was all too clear to English workmen that the refugees offered serious competition in their crafts and trades. And from the point of view of the City authorities, the widespread naturalization of refugees was something to be resisted fiercely because it threatened to denude their treasury of profitable dues which aliens had to pay.

On the other hand, by their actions and sufferings the Huguenots fleeing Louis XIV's France were demonstrating the strength of their Protestantism. Anti-Popery was the strongest emotive force of the day: strong enough to give credit to the wild accusations of Titus Oates and to fuel the hysteria surrounding his "Popish Plot"; strong enough to prolong the Exclusion Crisis for many bitter months; strong enough, in the end, for the Roman Catholic King James II to be removed from the English throne virtually without bloodshed. It was not easy for Protestant Londoners to express vigorous opposition towards the Huguenots when, at the time the *dragonnades* started, they were being warned that the future James II would prove to be "Queen Mary in breeches", or urged to support collections for the refugees because "you know

---

[17] Quoted in Michael Duffy, *The Englishman and the Foreigner* (Cambridge, 1986), p. 14.

Paris, Dec. 19. The 14th Inftant the Council of State made an Order forbidding the Exercife of the Proteftant Religion at *Lenquais* and *Bade-fou*, in the Diocefs of *Sarlatte*, and commanding, That the Proteftant Churches there fhould be forthwith Demolifhed. And from *Mompellier* we have an account, That the Duke *de Novailles*, the King's Lieutenant in *Languedoc*, had, upon the Orders he received from Court, executed the Decree of the Parliament of *Touloufe* for the Demolifh-ing the Proteftant Church at *Mompelier*. The Let-

PLATE 13: *The London Gazette reports attacks on Protestantism in France, 1682.*

not how soon your own condition may be the same with theirs" (Plate 13). It was even harder for them to do so when James was on the throne while, in France, the Revocation of the "perpetual and irrevocable" Edict of Nantes cemented their belief that trust could not be placed in Catholic kings.

Consequently the Huguenots were met at one and the same time by support and hostility, by encouragement and opposition. The public collections for them were strongly commended by the Bishop of London and his clergy, and met with a very generous response; but there were real or threatened riots against the French weavers in the eastern suburbs in 1675, 1681 and 1683, and opponents of a Bill for erecting a French church at St Martin Orgars argued that it would "create a perpetual settlement for foreigners in the heart of the city to the prejudice of our own merchants and traders, and endanger the bringing a charge on the city by poor". Charles II offered the refugees free denization, but the House of Commons – largely because of pressure from the London representatives – long resisted all attempts to pass an act of General Naturalization. While employers welcomed the craft skills of the Huguenots, the London Companies often failed to show understanding of the problems the refugees faced. A great volume of

PLATE 14:   Hogarth's "Noon" (1738). The congregation of L'Eglise des Grecs leaves church after a service, while native Londoners on the other side of the gutter pursue baser pleasures. Note the kite caught on the church roof, an allusion to the refugee origins of the congregation; the pastor in the doorway, with his sober Geneva bands; and the satirical comment on French dress.

pamphlet and newsletter literature showed sympathy to their cause, but there were also pamphlets like *Considerations upon the Mischiefs that may arise from granting too much Indulgence to Foreigners* (1735). Stereotypes about French dress, manners and eating habits persisted (Plate 14), and it was complained that the refugees' habit of "living much upon cabbage and roots" resulted in "noisome water" which gave offence.[18]

On balance, though, the only conclusion one can reach is that the Huguenots met a reception of genuine warmth. Every group of foreigners washed up on the shores of England has met opposition. What is striking about the Huguenot settlement is the minimal degree of antagonism that such an exceptionally large number of refugees encountered. Yet it could hardly be otherwise, when the evidence of real persecution was so strong and so close at hand:

> "Martha Guisard, living in Frith street, Soho ... will tell ... that she came out of France, because Jean Guisard, her father, was burnt at Nerac; being accused of having irreverently received the Host ...

> Let [people] ask of the Sieur Peyferié and his family, What made them abandon a great estate, to be reduced to great straits in Tower street, Soho? He will answer, That, being accused, with some neighbours of his, of having [had Divine Service] in his country house; he was condemned to be hanged: and his house demolished, and his woods destroyed. But God, of his mercy, delivered him from that danger ...

> The Sieurs Dupré, and Moise Du Boust, now living in the parish of Saint Giles in the Fields, will testify, That they were persecuted in their persons and their estates,

---

[18] *Reasons humbly offered by Several of the Principal Inhabitants of the Parish of St Martins Orgars London ...*, (undated broadside); *Proceedings of the Huguenot Society*, V (1894–6): 306.

[and] their houses demolished; before they fled into this country . . .

Mary Perreau, living in Spittlefields, will tell you, That she was married, at Plymouth, to Pierre Perreau, a French Pilot; who, a month after their marriage, being sailed for the Straits [of Gibraltar], was taken, and carried into France: where he was condemned to the Galleys for 101 years."[19]

---

[19] Hilary Reneu, *Preface to the Second English Translation (1707) of Jean Claude's Les Plaintes des Protestants cruellement opprimés dans le Royaume de France,* reprinted in Edward Arber (ed.), *The Torments of Protestant Slaves . . .* (London, 1908), pp. 419–420.

The Huguenots and English Banking and Commerce

Apart from religious considerations, Londoners were also disposed to accept the refugees in the 1680s and 1690s because they believed their presence provided economic opportunities. They knew that the Walloons and Huguenots who had arrived earlier had made a considerable impact, as was proved by the wealth of the descendants of such families as Delmé, Desbouveries, Dubois, Houblon, Le Keux, Lethieullier, Lordell and Papillon. They knew, too, that the new arrivals included men with useful international contacts and a sprinkling of people with experience in *rentes* and other advanced financial dealings on the Continent.

The burden of two lengthy wars with France between 1689 and 1713 was enormous, and could not have been sustained without major changes in the structure of English finance which have been described as adding up to a "financial revolution". Both the descendants of the older refugees and the new arrivals played an important role. Essential to the "revolution" was the foundation of the Bank of England in 1694; seven of its initial Directors, including the Governor, Sir John Houblon, were of Walloon or Huguenot extraction, and the wealthier refugees were quick to deposit money. It is known that £104,000 of the first £1,200,000 was provided by 123 recently arrived Huguenots. They may have also contributed something like a tenth of the investment in other early English Funds, though this is a matter of debate.[20] Jean Castaing's

---

[20] A. C. Carter, *Getting, Spending and Investing in Early Modern Times* (Assen, 1975); F. M. Crouzet, "Walloons, Huguenots and the Bank of England", *Proceedings of the Huguenot Society*, XXV (1989–93): 167–78.

PLATE 15: *Bank note from Minet and Fector's Dover bank, 1797, payable at Dover or at the bank's London house of business in Austin Friars.*

The Course of the Exchange, providing weekly stock quotations, was the forerunner of today's Stock Exchange Official List.

Other economic changes taking place around 1700 included the widening of the scope and extent of England's trade, and early insurance ventures. Again the French refugees had much to offer. Their international connections, especially in the silk and wine trades, helped open up new fields; and they provided some 15 per cent of the backing for the London Assurance Company in 1720, a figure subsequently rising to peak at just under 25 per cent by 1743.[21] As bankers, as merchants and in insurance, Huguenots remained prominent throughout the eighteenth century, such names as Aubert, Bosanquet, Cazalet, Gaussen, Janssen, Lambert, Loubier and Minet becoming well-known and respected in London life (Plate 15).

---

[21] *Proceedings of the Huguenot Society,* XIX (1952–8): 325–6.

The Huguenots and Weaving

The Huguenot contribution to the weaving trade that came to be based on Spitalfields, and especially to silk-weaving, is rightly well known. The London silk industry was founded by refugees from the Low Countries and France during the reign of Elizabeth I. Those who came from Walloon areas and (to a lesser extent) France became increasingly dominant in a trade, then based particularly on Bishopsgate, which may have involved a fifth of all stranger households in London by 1593. It seems that in the sixteenth century, as indeed still in the eighteenth, many of those who became silk weavers in London were not so before their arrival but adapted skills from related trades to silk weaving after they had come to England. On the other hand, the Court Books of the Weavers' Company show that experts in the 1680s agreed that some new Huguenot refugees from Languedoc possessed skills never previously demonstrated in England.[22]

Weaving was a major craft skill common to all the phases of Protestant refugee immigration into London. Weavers carried their skill in their heads and their hands, so it could travel with them. Because most craftsmen did not need to worry about abandoning expensive plant or land holdings, they could run the risks of leaving their homeland with a certain degree of security and peace of mind. The craft's mobility was a major reason why weavers from overseas had traditionally been employed in large numbers long before the Reformation, certainly

---

[22] Lien Bich Luu, "French-speaking refugees and the foundation of the London silk industry in the 16th century", *Proceedings of the Huguenot Society*, XXVI (1994–7): 564ff; Robin D. Gwynn, *Huguenot Heritage* (1985), p. 69.

since the fourteenth century, when Edward III had encouraged Flemish weavers to settle in England. But it is also clear that weavers were particularly strongly represented among continental Protestants, as they also were among English Lollards; they seem to have had a tradition of thinking for themselves, and to have been open to Reformed ideas in a way that other occupational groups like coopers were not. Many of the stranger silk workers who arrived in Elizabethan London did so for religious reasons,[23] and we have seen how, a century later, weavers formed the core of the east London Huguenot community which adhered so steadfastly to continental forms of Protestant worship.

Weaving was a skilled and labour-intensive occupation. Most Huguenot weavers would simply have contributed to the available pool of labour in London, although they may have been superior workers because of their proven determination and the motivation to succeed forced on them by their urgent need. But some offered genuinely new skills, particularly in combining different materials. In the late Elizabethan period mention was made of the "abundance which the strangers make of tuff taffetas, wrought velvets, figured satins and other sorts of silk mingled with thread and wool". The workmanship whose novelty so impressed the Court of Weavers nearly a century later involved a demonstration taking a piece of English-made alamode silk, then producing it "shot with a piece of coloured silk". Such skills could create new fashions – and new markets. A celebrated case of the 1690s in which the refugee Etienne Seignoret and others were impeached, convicted and heavily fined by Parliament for illegally trading with France during wartime shows just how high were the stakes involved in the silk trade.

---

[23] Andrew Pettegree, *Foreign Protestant Communities*, ch. 4; Luu, "French-speaking refugees", p. 567.

The Spitalfields silk industry prospered in the early eighteenth century; its exports to America grew, the increasing number of Londoners provided a developing market, and the main previous centre of competition in England, Canterbury, declined. Huguenot participation in the industry and the area remained very strong until after mid-century. When in 1745 the leading inhabitants of Spitalfields underlined their loyalty to the Crown in the face of the threat of Bonnie Prince Charlie and the Jacobites, the *London Gazette* printed a list of their names together with the number of their workmen and dependants ready to serve King George. It shows both the number and the economic power of the Huguenot masters, who between them offered some 2000 men. Those offering a dozen or more included:

Captain James Dalbiac	80	Daniel Pineau	29
Peter Campart	74	Peter Abraham Ogier	
Daniel Gobbee	70	and Sons	28
Lewis Chauvet	65	James Lardant	27
Godin and Ogier	60	Peter Bourdon	26
Abraham Jeudwine	60	Simon Dalbiac, jr.	25
John Rondeau	57	Nicholas Hebert	25
Peter Auber and Son	52	James Maze	25
Benjamin Champion	50	James Maze	24
Peter Ougier	50	Peter Delamare and Co.	22
Daniel Pilon	49	Peter Maillard	21
John Luke Landon	48	James Gautier	20
Daniel Mesman	48	Jacob Jamet	20
Abraham Deheul	47	John Batcheler	19
Daniel le Vautier	47	Lewis Desormeaux	19
Obadiah Agace and Sons	41	James Ouvry	19
Samuel Alavoine	39	Peter Lekeux	18
Lewis Chevelier	38	John Maze	17
Samuel Savage	36	James Pigne	17
Chantrey & Co.	35	James Roberdeau	17
John Ouvry	35	James Auber	16
John Sabatier	34	John Ogier	16
Daniel Cabbinell	30	Riviete and Ogier	16
Bigot and De Lavau	30	Paul Auder	14

Ann Barbutt	14	Isaac Dupree	12
Abraham Ravenel	14	Peter Duthoit, sr.	12
Judith Sequeret and		Gabriel Grillier	12
Bourdillion	14	John Lamy	12

In all some three-fifths of those who promised men had foreign names, and they promised about twice as many men as the English manufacturers signing the same declaration.[24]

Could we be wafted back in time to walk the streets of eighteenth-century London, we would find that Spitalfields looked and sounded different from the rest of the city. There were three reasons for its distinctive appearance: its comparative newness, since it was only in the second half of the seventeenth century that open fields had been transformed into housing; its Huguenot settlement, for the weavers kept gardens and were noted for their fondness for flowers; and the weaving craft itself, which meant that many houses came later to have garrets in the roofs. The weavers' looms could chatter loudly, and it has been suggested that silk waste found used as packing in the floorboards of houses in Spital Square was there to deaden the sound of the looms overhead.[25] However the noise that most struck Englishmen came from the caged canary birds that sang while the weavers worked. One opponent of general naturalization found them the inspiration for his *Canary-Birds Naturaliz'd in Utopia. A Canto* (1709):

> Here they grew fat, and liv'd at Ease,
> And bigger look'd than Refugees;
> Kindly protected from the Stroke
> Of swift persuing Gallick Hawk.

---

[24] *Proceedings of the Huguenot Society*, II (1887–88), 453–6 and XX (1958–64), 76; *The Quiet Conquest: the Huguenots 1685 to 1985* (Museum of London, 1985), p. 98.
[25] *Survey of London volume XXVII: Spitalfields and Mile End New Town* (London, 1957), p. 55.

Them we so well did entertain,
They would not choose go Home again,
But now at last so sawcy grew,
That to aspiring Heights they flew:
They must be topping Masters made,
And, as our free-born Subjects, trade.

The Huguenots and other London Crafts and Professions

Aside from weaving, the range of other crafts and professions in which the Huguenots made their mark was remarkably broad. Glass, printing, bookbinding and medicine were all fields in which the refugees who came in late Tudor times excelled. Jean Carré of Arras fled from religious riots in Antwerp in 1567 and established a glasshouse near the Tower of London which produced crystal glass for fine drinking vessels; he was responsible for bringing to London another Antwerp Protestant, Jacob Verzelini, under whose supervision the glasshouse prospered (Plate 16). Thomas Vautrollier was an outstanding printer working in Elizabethan London, and Jean de Planche an accomplished binder (Plate 17). Doctors who crossed the Channel included Pierre Chamberlen, the inventor of the obstetric forceps, Sir Théodore de Mayerne and Guillaume de Laune. De Laune's son, Gideon, played an important part in the foundation and early history of the Society of Apothecaries.

One obvious potential career for educated refugees was teaching, although few were so adept at delightful self-advertisement as Claude de Sainliens, a Bourbon gentleman who arrived in London in 1564 and taught a generation of Elizabethans:

> In Paules Church yard, at the
> signe of the golden ball: there is a Frenchman,
> which teacheth both the tongues:
> that is the Latine, and French:
> and which doth his dutie . . .

PLATE 16:   *Brownish crystal glass engraved with diamond-point. Produced in the London glasshouse of Jacob Verzelini, dated 1581.*

PLATE 17:   *John de Planche, binding of the Four Gospels, in Anglo-Saxon, 1571, with arms of Queen Elizabeth I.*

John, how is thy maister called?

He is called M. Claudius Holyband.

Is he maried? what countreyman is he?

He is a Frenchman: he hath a wife and children.

God save you Sir.[26]

The Huguenot refugees of a century later also included many schoolmasters, but they were more prominent in new directions. Hardly a single aspect of artistic, cultural, fashionable and scientific life was unaffected by them. They and their descendants included actors (David Garrick graced the London stage), painters (Louis Cheron influenced the Academy of Painting in St Martin's Lane) and musicians (the organist and composer Peter Prelleur started his career as a writing master in Spitalfields). They became involved in every kind of personal ornamentation as hairdressers and wigmakers, jewellers, makers of clothing and shoes. The furniture and designs of Daniel Marot (Plate 18), Jean Pelletier and Jean Tijou (Plate 19) helped change the feel of great houses and public places: eventually the designs – and the Huguenots' love for gardens – would influence lesser homes too. Some refugees showed a rare talent for making precision instruments like guns (de Gruchy, Monlong) (Plate 20), telescopes (Dollond), and watches (Amyot, de Beauffre, Lestourgeon).

The particular centre for expensive fashionable wares lay in the west of the capital. If the traveller walking through early eighteenth-century Spitalfields would have heard French spoken and canary birds singing, when he reached Westminster he would have been breathing in French culture in an English milieu. Perhaps he would have paused to refresh himself at the French eating houses in Pall Mall or the baths in Long Acre noted in the earliest London

---

[26] Claudius Holyband, *The French Littelton: the edition of 1609* (Cambridge, 1953), pp. 8, 10.

THE SPEAKER'S STATE COACH.

PLATE 18: *The State Coach of the Speaker of the House of Commons, originally designed for King William III by Daniel Marot, 1698.*

PLATE 19: *Wrought-iron balustrade, probably by Jean Tijou, from 35 Lincoln's Inn Fields. Early eighteenth century.*

guidebook for foreign visitors.[27] Later in the century he might have continued his travels by crossing Westminster Bridge, designed by Charles Labelye in 1738.

Because the art of the goldsmith is enduring, it is in that field that the Huguenot contribution of the late seventeenth and early eighteenth centuries remains today most immediately visible. The Georgian silver emanating from London is beautiful, and much of the best was produced by such Huguenot craftsmen as Pierre Archambaut (father and son), Augustin and Samuel Courtauld, Paul Crespin, Pierre Harache (father and son), Paul de Lamerie, Isaac Liger, Jacob and Samuel Margas, Pierre Platel and David Willaume. Not only was their workmanship outstanding, but they

[27] F. Colsoni, *Le Guide de Londres* (1693), ed. Walter H. Godfrey (Cambridge, for the London Topographical Society, 1951), pp. 16–17, 63–4.

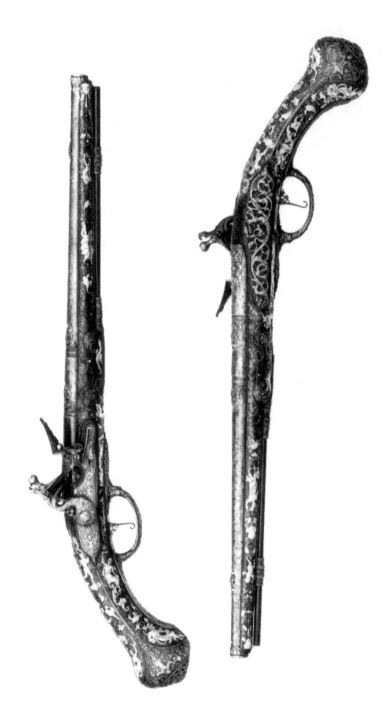

PLATE 20:   *Pair of flintlock holster pistols by Pierre Monlong, c. 1695.*

PLATE 21:   *Silver-gilt ewer by Pierre Harache the younger, hallmarked 1705–6. This is a fine example of the distinctive helmet-shaped ewer, a form introduced into England by the Huguenots.*

introduced new forms of silverware that Englishmen had not previously seen, such as the soup tureen, Louis Mettayer's bowls, and the helmet-shaped ewer (Plate 21).

Assimilation

One reason why the Huguenots made such an impact was that Londoners were predisposed to accept Parisian fashions as being in the best taste. Englishmen had accepted that France set the standard which others strove to emulate. London felt-makers complained that they were put out of work through the success of the "Cordeback (being *a la mode de France*) . . . being generally worn because of the name both by rich and poor". ("Cordeback" was derived from Caudebec in Normandy, just as our modern "denim" derived from "de Nîmes".) Other native artisans found themselves confronted by the same problem. "The English have now so great an esteem for the work-manship of the French refugees that hardly anything vends with-out a gallic name", it was being said within fifteen years of the Revocation.

Nevertheless, while the ability to work in the French style was an asset, there were sound reasons why the Huguenots should have wanted to become assimilated into English society speedily. Many of their leaders implicitly urged it; already by the first decade of the eighteenth century Jean Armand Dubourdieu, minister at the Savoy, was scorning those refugees who still had "les fleurs de lis gravées dans le coeur".[28] After the failure of the Treaty of Utrecht (1713) to include a clause allow-ing them back into France, there remained little realistic prospect that they could return home; their future lay in an English-speak-ing environment. Moreover England frequently found herself at war with France during the eighteenth century, and it was

---

[28] Quoted in Myriam Yardeni, *Le Refuge Protestant* (Paris, 1985), p. 124.

not in the interests of the refugees or their descendants to have their loyalty questioned. Perhaps that is why, amidst one period of tension with France, Abraham De la Neuvemaison decided to sign his name as Abraham Newhouse, after his family had been settled in England for several generations, even when writing for fellow Huguenot descendants (Plate 22). Within three or four generations, assimilation was largely complete. Names often became anglicized or distorted in the process, while intermarriage with English people became the rule rather than, as amongst first generation refugees, the exception. The Huguenot refugees of the sixteenth and seventeenth century had become English. It was perfectly appropriate that the 1803 Napoleonic War "Declaration of the Merchants, Bankers, Traders, and other Inhabitants of London" that they would "stand or fall with our King and Country" should be signed by a chairman, Jacob Bosanquet, whose grandfather had been born in Lunel and granted denization as a Huguenot refugee in England in 1687 (Plate 23).

In institutional terms, assimilation meant that bodies established on a French regional foundation were superseded by ones of a more national character. Between 1683 and 1710 many Friendly Societies were formed in London like the Society of Dauphiné, the Society of Lintot [Normandy], or the Society of Parisians, emphasising the local areas in France from which the refugees had come. Such societies provided poor relief as well as retaining a memory of shared roots. The earliest, the "Société des Enfants de Nîmes", for example, charged each member a shilling per quarter for the relief of its poor, and ensured that it would remain firmly for people from Nîmes, St Cezaire, Cayfargues, Bouillargues, Courbessac and the surrounding countryside by charging any foreigner wishing to join £10 – two hundred times the shilling entry fee for those from the Nîmes region. The

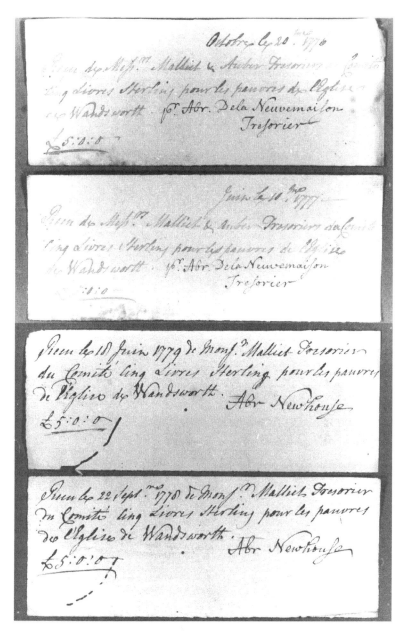

PLATE 22: *Abraham de la Neuvemaison, an elder and treasurer of the French Church of Wandsworth, becomes Abraham Newhouse. Four successive annual receipts to the body administering national poor relief to the Huguenots, 1776–9.*

LONDON, JULY 26, 1803.

THE DECLARATION

OF THE

Merchants, Bankers,

TRADERS, and other INHABITANTS

OF LONDON AND ITS NEIGHBOURHOOD.

AT a very numerous Meeting of MERCHANTS, BANKERS, TRADERS, and other INHABITANTS of LONDON and its Neighbourhood, held on the ROYAL EXCHANGE this Day, in Consequence of public Advertisement,

The following DECLARATION was proposed, and unanimously resolved upon:—

WE, the Merchants, Bankers, Traders, and other Inhabitants of London and its Neighbourhood, deem it our bounden Duty, at the present momentous Period, to make public our *unanimous* Determination to *stand* or *fall* with our *King and Country.*

The Independence and Existence of the British Empire—the Safety, the Liberty, the Life of every Man in the Kingdom are at Stake. The Events perhaps of a few Months, *certainly* of a few Years, are to determine whether *we* and our Children are to continue *Freemen* and *Members* of the most flourishing Community in the World, or whether we are to be the *Slaves* of our most implacable Enemies—*themselves* the *Slaves* of a foreign Usurper?

We look on this great Crisis without Dismay We have the most firm Reliance on the Spirit and Virtue of the People of this Country. We believe that there exists a firmer as well as nobler Courage than any which Rapine can inspire; and that we cannot entertain such gloomy and unworthy Apprehensions of the moral Order of the World, as to think that *so* admirable a Quality can be the *exclusive* Attribute of Freebooters or Slaves. We fight for our *Laws* and *Liberties*—to defend the *dearest* Hopes of our *Children*—to maintain the unspotted Glory which we have inherited from our Ancestors—to guard from Outrage and Shame those whom Nature has entrusted to our Protection—to preserve the Honour and Existence of the Country that gave us Birth.

We fight for that Constitution and System of Society, which is at once the noblest Monument and the firmest Bulwark of Civilization!—We fight to preserve the *whole* Earth from the barbarous Yoke of military Despotism!—We fight for the Independence of all Nations, even of those who are the most indifferent to our Fate, or the most blindly jealous of our Prosperity!

In so *glorious* a Cause—in the Defence of these dear and sacred Objects, we trust that the God of our Fathers will inspire us with a *Valour* which will be more than equal to the daring Ferocity of those who are lured, by the Hope of Plunder, to fight the Battles of Ambition.

His Majesty is about to call upon his People to arm in their own Defence. We *trust*, and we *believe* that he will *not* call on them in *vain*—that the Freemen of this Land, going forth in the righteous Cause of their Country, under the Blessing of Almighty God, will inflict the most signal Chastisement on those who have dared to threaten our Destruction—a Chastisement, of which the Memory will long guard the Shores of this Island, and which may not only vindicate the Honour, and establish the Safety of the British Empire, but may also, to the latest Posterity, serve as an Example to strike Terror into Tyrants, and to give Courage and Hope to insulted and oppressed Nations.

For the Attainment of these *great* Ends, it is necessary that we should not only be an *unanimous*, but a *zealous*, and *ardent*, and *unconquerable* People—that we should consider the public Safety as the chief Interest of every Individual—that every Man should deem the Sacrifice of his Fortune and his Life to his Country as nothing more than his Duty—that no Man should murmur at any Exertions or Privations which this *awful* Crisis may impose upon him—that we should regard Faintness or Languor in the *common* Cause as the basest Treachery—that we should go into the Field with an unshaken Resolution to *conquer* or to *die*—and that we should look upon nothing as a Calamity compared with the Subjugation of our Country.

We have most sacred Duties to perform—we have most invaluable Blessings to preserve—we have to *gain* Glory and Safety, or to incur indelible Disgrace, and to fall into irretrievable Ruin. Upon *our* Efforts will depend the Triumph of Liberty over Despotism—of rational Independence over Projects of universal Empire—and, finally, of Civilization itself over Barbarism.

At *such* a Moment we deem it our Duty solemnly to bind ourselves to each other, and to our Countrymen, in the most sacred Manner, that we will employ all our Exertions to rouse the *Spirit*, and to assist the Resources of the Kingdom—that we will be ready with our Services of *every* Sort, and on *every* Occasion, in its Defence—and that we will rather perish together, than live to see the Honour of the British Name tarnished, or that *noble* Inheritance of *Greatness*, Glory, and Liberty destroyed, which has descended to us from our Forefathers, and which we are determined to transmit to our Posterity.

JACOB BOSANQUET, CHAIRMAN.

PLATE 23: *1803 Declaration of London merchants and others, signed by Jacob Bosanquet as chairman, to "stand or fall with our King and Country" because "the independence and existence of the British Empire" was at stake.*

PLATE 24:   *The French Hospital near Old Street.*

Society's inaugural rules laid down that the prosperity of the City of London, as well as the royal family, was to be toasted at its annual feast.[29]

Although the Huguenots maintained for a time a French regional patriotism in the suburbs of London, it gradually dissipated, and refugee institutions tended to become simply "French". Before the end of the seventeenth century Houses of Charity had been established in Soho and Spitalfields to act as foodbanks for refugees regardless of their place of origin. According to William Maitland's *History of London* (1739), the Spitalfields House of Charity ("the Soup") then distributed provisions to nearly three hundred poor families:

> Some receiving two Portions per Week, others three, or four, and the most necessitous six: Each Portion consists of

[29] *Establissement de la Societé des Enfans de Nismes* (London, 1683).

PLATE 25:   *Seal of* La Providence, *showing Elijah being fed by the ravens under the legend "Dominus Providebit" – "God will provide".*

a Pan of good Broth, mixed with six Ounces of Bread, half a Pound of Meat, and the same Weight of good Bread.

The French Protestant Hospital, *La Providence* (Plates 24, 25) was founded near Old Street and Bath Street in 1718 to care particularly for the elderly and infirm, and at its eighteenth-century peak cared for well over 200 residents. It still exists, now in Rochester, in the form of flatlets for old people.

Schools were also established. Best known is the Westminster French Protestant School, which came into being in 1747 (Plate 26):

> The school was situated in Windmill Street, Tottenham Court Road, a street much favoured by physicians for its good air. It occupied two houses and a garden ... In 1829 the school moved to another house in the same street, and, in 1846, to Westminster. The number of pupils was never very large, 30 (15 boys and 15 girls) in 1759, with 46 on the waiting list ... The children were apprenticed when they left school at the age of 14, and their apprentice Indentures give us an idea of the type of trades carried on in London towards the end of the eighteenth century. The boys

PLATE 26: *Receipt issued by the Westminster French Protestant School, 1791. As the receipt shows, the school at first educated both boys and girls; later it became restricted to girls alone. It closed in the 1920s. The children hold scriptural references to Psalm 27: 10 ("When my father and my mother forsake me, then the Lord will take me up") and Matthew 18: 14 ("It is not the will of your Father which is in heaven, that one of these little ones should perish").*

entered the trades of jeweller, apothecary, perruquier, watch-maker, weaver, musical and mathematical instrument maker, "imprimeur en tailles-douces", ebeniste, sculpteur, "doreur", "ciseleur", enameller. The girls mostly went as children's nurses. The Anniversary Service and Sermon was the great event of the school year, when the children sang the old French psalms.[30]

---

[30] Grace L. Gwynn, "The Huguenot Settlements in London", special number of *Le Lien* (Eglise Protestante Française de Londres, n.d.), pp. 9–10.

PLATE 27: *The present French Church of London, Soho Square, from an engraving made at its opening in 1893. Designed by Aston Webb with a mixture of Gothic and Romanesque features, it was built in plum-coloured brick with light red terracotta tiles and green roof slates.*

The school has gone, but has been succeeded by a Foundation which offers assistance towards the secondary and tertiary education of children of Huguenot descent.

Assimilation also meant fewer French churches; as against 28 in London and its environs in 1700, by 1800 there were only eight and by 1900, just three. Today only one remains, the former Threadneedle Street congregation, now located in Soho Square (Plate 27) and meeting the religious needs not of the descendants of refugees but of modern French Protestant residents in London.

Appendix: A Visitor's Guide to Huguenot London

A great variety of enduring attractions of Huguenot interest await the visitor to London willing to look them out. Some have already been mentioned in this book, others have not. Some are situated in buildings and museums that every traveller is likely to visit, others require effort to track down. Here is a selection of the more accessible, listed alphabetically by institution or location:

The *British Museum* has notable items of Huguenot interest including silver and glass.

Walking up Croom's Hill in *Greenwich*, it is possible to envisage what life might have been like for the wealthier descendants of the refugees. Ratebooks show that in Georgian times it was the home of a community including such Huguenot families as Breholt, Delamotte, Ducarrel (at no. 14), Girardot, Guigier, Lapostre, Layard, Olivier, Savary and Teulon. At the bottom of the hill, the graveyard includes a prominent monument to Sir John Lethieullier (1632–1718). Nearby the Old Royal Observatory has fine examples of eighteenth-century Dollond telescopes, and the National Maritime Museum houses portraits of J. T. Desaguliers and Edward Riou and a journal kept by a ship's captain during the La Rochelle expedition of 1628.

Hampton Court Palace has fine boundary screens by Jean Tijou, and within the Royal Apartments will be found a chimney piece by Le Sage, paintings by Rousseau and Van Somer, furniture in the style of Daniel Marot, and Pelletier carving.

Near *Leicester Square and Piccadilly Circus*, the Congregational Chapel in Orange Street was formerly used for French Protestant worship. Not far away, the French church building in West Street (1700–43) is "now a ballet school – but with an exterior still very obviously Huguenot" [*Proceedings of the Huguenot Society*, XXVI (1994–7), 594].

The *Museum of London* has many notable items of Huguenot interest, including watches. They can be identified from the magnificent *Quiet Conquest* exhibition catalogue published by this Museum in 1985 (see the Bibliography which follows this appendix).

St Paul's Cathedral contains gates by Jean Tijou and, at the west end of the crypt, a memorial to Captain Edward Riou R.N.

Soho Square is the home of the French Protestant Church of London today. The building was designed by Aston Webb, who was also responsible for Admiralty Arch and the Mall. Note the modern doorway tympanum representing the Huguenot refugee experience. In keeping with Reformed practice the church has no altar, but a centrally placed communion table and a prominent pulpit. For details of the church and its modern history, see Yves Jaulmes, *The French Protestant Church of London and the Huguenots*. The next-door house no. 10, one of the two surviving original houses in Soho Square, was probably the home of the Huguenot painter Jacques Rousseau (died 1693).

The weavers' lofts of *Spitalfields* with their windows, probably added some time after the houses were first built, remain a distinctive feature of the area. Some striking Georgian houses in Elder, Fournier and Princelet Streets have been restored and many have Huguenot connections. Note the date 1725 on the guttering of 27 Fournier Street, originally built for the Huguenot weaver Pierre Bourdon and by 1759 occupied by Obadiah Agace. 19 Princelet Street (built 1718) was the eighteenth-century home of Pierre Abraham Ogier. 56 Artillery Lane is a rare example of a surviving Georgian shop front; together with no. 58, it was owned in 1757 by

Nicholas Jourdain, a director of the French Protestant Hospital *La Providence*. Substantial houses like these were of course built for master weavers (i.e. employers), not for the ordinary run of poor workers. The Great Mosque on the corner of Brick Lane and Fournier Street was originally built as a Huguenot church in 1743 (see above, pp. 18–20).

The *Victoria and Albert Museum* has notable items of Huguenot interest including silk and ceramics.

Westminster Abbey houses sculptures by Roubiliac, effigies by Maximilien Poultrain or Colt and by Le Sueur, and memorials to Field-Marshal Ligonier, Isaac Casaubon, David Garrick and (of special interest to American visitors) Major John André.

The work by Batisse in the Bibliography that follows is also evocative with regard to Huguenot London, but some of the connections he makes are unproven.

Select Bibliography

François Batisse, *Londres Huguenot: sur les pas des Huguenots Français à travers Londres*, (Eglise Protestante Française de Londres, 1978).

Margaret Cox, "Huguenots of Spitalfields: the evidence from the Christ Church Project", *Proceedings of the Huguenot Society of Great Britain and Ireland*, XXV (1989–93): 21–38.

Ole Peter Grell, "The French and Dutch congregations in London in the early 17th century", *Proceedings of the Huguenot Society of Great Britain and Ireland*, XXIV (1983–8): 362–77.

——, J. I. Israel and N. Tyacke (eds), *From Persecution to Toleration: the Glorious Revolution in England*, (Clarendon Press, Oxford, 1991) (includes Andrew Pettegree, "The French and Walloon Communities in London, 1550–1688", and Robin D. Gwynn, "Disorder and Innovation: the reshaping of the French churches of London after the Glorious Revolution").

Robin D. Gwynn, "The Distribution of Huguenot Refugees in England, II: London and its environs", *Proceedings of the Huguenot Society of London*, XXII (1970–6): 509–67.

——, *Huguenot Heritage: the history and contribution of the Huguenots in Britain*, (Routledge & Kegan Paul, 1985).

Yves Jaulmes, *The French Protestant Church of London and the Huguenots* (Eglise Protestante Française de Londres, 1993) [pamphlet].

London County Council, *Survey of London*, especially vols. 27 (Spitalfields) and 33–34 (St. Anne, Soho).

C. F. A. Marmoy, "The Huguenots and their Descendants in East London", *East London Papers*, XIII no. 2 (1970–1): 72–88.

William Minet, "Notes on the Threadneedle Street Registers" (unpublished typescript in the Huguenot Library, University College, London, n.d.).

Andrew Pettegree, *Foreign Communities in Sixteenth-Century London* (Clarendon Press, Oxford, 1986).

Besides articles specifically listed here, the *Proceedings of the Huguenot Society of Great Britain and Ireland* (formerly *of London*) contain many others including [volume given in Roman numerals] pieces on City of London Records on the Huguenots [VII], the French Charity School of Westminster [XII, XIII], the French Protestant hospital *La Providence* [VI, VII, XV, XXI, XXII], the Spitalfields *Maison de Charité* [XXIII], Huguenot Gunmakers and Watchmakers of London [XX and XXVI respectively], Huguenots in the London financial world [XV, XIX, XXV], in the London silk industry [XV, XX, XXVII], in the London book trade [XXV] and in the London Trained Bands [XV], and London-based Huguenot Friendly Societies [VI,VIII]. There are also articles of variable quality by W. H. Manchée on regions of "Huguenot London" [X, XI, XII, XIII, XIV, XVII]. The majority of essays in volume 26 no. 2 of the *Proceedings* (1995), a special number in memory of Irene Scouloudi, concern aspects of Huguenot settlement in London.

The Quiet Conquest: the Huguenots 1685 to 1985 (Museum of London, 1985).

Irene Scouloudi, "Alien Immigration into and Alien Communities in London, 1558–1640", *Proceedings of the Huguenot Society of London*, XVI (1937–41): 27–49; but much fuller and still valuable is her unpublished London University M.Sc. (Econ.) thesis (1937) .

—— (ed.), *Huguenots in Britain and their French Background, 1550–1800*, (Macmillan Press, 1987).

R. A. Shaw, R. D. Gwynn and P. Thomas, *Huguenots in Wandsworth* (Wandsworth Borough Council, 1985) [pamphlet].

Francis H. W. Sheppard, "The Huguenots in Spitalfields and Soho", *Proceedings of the Huguenot Society of London*, XXI (1965–70), 355–65.

J. T. Squire, "The Huguenots at Wandsworth . . . ", *Proceedings of the Huguenot Society of London*, I (1885–86): 229–42, 261–312.

Laura Hunt Yungblut, *Strangers settled here amongst us: policies, perceptions and the presence of aliens in Elizabethan England* (Routledge, 1996).

Since being founded over a century ago, the Huguenot Society of Great Britain and Ireland (formerly the Huguenot Society of London) has seen to the publication, in its Quarto Series, of all known surviving registers of French churches in and about London:

Volume(s)	Church(es)
9, 13, 16, 21, 23	Threadneedle Street.
11	La Patente, Spitalfields.
22, 26	Savoy, Spring Gardens and Les Grecs.
25	Le Carré and Berwick Street.
28	Chapel Royal, St James, and Swallow Street.
29	The Tabernacle, Glasshouse Street, and Leicester Fields.
30	Rider Court.
31	Hungerford Market, later Castle Street.
32	Le Petit Charenton, West Street, Pearl Street, and Crispin Street.
37	St Martin Orgars.

39	St Jean, Spitalfields.
42	The Artillery.
45	Wheeler Street, Swanfields, Hoxton, La Patente (Soho), Répertoire Général.

Other volumes in the same series are also of direct London relevance:

10, 57	Returns of Aliens Resident in London, Henry VIII to Charles I.
33	Extracts from the Court Books of the Weavers' Company of London 1610–1730.
37	Includes histories of the churches of St Martin Orgars and Swallow Street.
38, 48, 58	Minutes of the Consistory of the Threadneedle Street church, 1560–5, 1571–7, 1679–92 (the first and last of these have significant historical introductions).
49	Relief of refugees 1681–7.
50, 51	Handlists of the archives of the French Church of London and of records in the Huguenot Library.
52, 53	Records of the French Protestant Hospital.
54	Calendar of the letter books of the French Church of London 1643–59.
55	Case-book of the Spitalfields *Maison de Charité*, 1739–41.

Index

Agace, Obadiah and Sons 37, 59
Alavoine, Samuel 37
America 24, 26, 37
Amyot 43
André, Major John 60
Apothecaries, Society of 40
Archambaut, Pierre 45
Auber 37
Aubert 34
Auder, Paul 38

Bank of England 33
Barbutt, Ann 38
Batcheler, John 37
Battersea 23
de Beauffre 43
Bigot 37
Bishopsgate 35
bookbinding 40, 42
Bosanquet 34, 50, 52
Bourdillion 38
Bourdon, Peter 37, 59
Breholt 22, 58
Briot, Nicholas 13
British Museum 58

Cabbinell, Daniel 37
Calvin, John 9
Campart, Peter 37
canary birds 38
Canterbury 4, 37
Carré, Jean 40
Casaubon, Isaac 60
Castaing, Jean 33
de Caus, Isaac 13
Cazalet 34
cemetery 23

Chamberlen, Pierre 40
Champion, Benjamin 37
Channel Islands 22
Chantrey & Co 37
Charles I 11
Charles II 11, 12, 13, 29
Chauvet, Lewis 37
Chelsea 22
Cheron, Louis 43
Chesterfield, Lord 17
Chevelier, Lewis 37
Church of England 9, 13, 17
Civil War 11, 13
Colt, see Poultrain
Commons, House of 29, 44
Compton, Henry, Bishop of London
    24, 27, 29
Courtauld 45
craftsmen 14–15, 28–29, 40ff, 49
Crespin, Paul 45

Dalbiac 37
Deheul, Abraham 37
Delamare, Peter and Co. 37
Delamotte 23, 58
Delmé 33
Desaguliers, J.T. 58
Desbouveries 33
Desormeaux, Lewis 37
Dissenters 11
Dollond 43, 58
Dover 7, 34
Dragonnades 8, 12, 28
Dubois 12, 33
Dubourdieu, Jean Armand 49
Du Boust, Moise 31
Ducarrel 23, 58

Dupré 31
Dupree, Isaac 38
Dutch in London 4, 5, 9–10, 27
Duthoit, Peter 38
dyers 23

Edward VI 4, 9
Elizabeth I 3, 9, 35, 42
d'Espagne, Jean 13
Evelyn, John 22
Exclusion Crisis 12, 28

feltmakers 23, 49
Fire of London 10, 28
Firmin, Thomas 24, 27
fishermen 24
Fontaine, Jaques and family 25–6
Fontaine, John 26
French Church of London, see
   Threadneedle Street
French Church of the Savoy, see
   Savoy
French Protestant Hospital, see *La
   Providence*
Friendly Societies 50, 53

des Gallars, Nicolas 9
gardeners 22, 38, 43
Garrick, David 43, 60
Gaussen 34
Gautier, James 37
Girardot 23, 58
glassmakers 22, 40–1
Gobbee, Daniel 37
Godin 37
goldsmiths 45, 47–8
Greenwich 22–3, 58
Grillier, Gabriel 38
Grosley, J. P. 27
de Gruchy 43
Guigier 23, 58
Guisard 31

Hampton Court 58
Harache, Pierre 45, 47
hatmakers 23
Hebert, Nicholas 37
Hérault, Louis 11, 13
Hogarth 17, 30
Holyband, see Sainliens
Houblon 33
Houses of Charity 21, 53–4
Hoxton 22
Huguenot, definition 3–4
Huguenot Society of Great Britain
   and Ireland viii, 62
Huguenots, assimilation 4, 17, 49ff
Huguenots in flight 6–8, 31–2, 35
Huguenots, loyalty to English crown
   37–8, 50, 52, 53
Huguenots, numbers 4, 8, 9, 15

insurance 34
Ipswich 24
Islington 22

Jamet, Jacob 37
James II 28
Janssen 34
Jeudwine, Abraham 37
Jourdain, Nicholas 60

La Providence 53–4, 60
Labelye, Charles 45
Lambert 34
Lambeth 23
de Lamerie, Paul 45
Lamy, John 38
Landon, John Luke 37
Lapostre 23, 58
Lardant, James 37
de Laune 40
de Lavau 37
Layard 23, 58
Leicester Square 58

Le Keux (Lekeux) 33, 37
Le Sage 58
Lestourgeon 43
Le Sueur 60
Lethieullier 33, 58
Liger, Isaac 45
Ligonier, Field-Marshal 60
London Assurance Company 34
London, character 1–3, 38, 43
London, significance as refugee centre 2, 4–5, 24–6
Long Acre 43
Lordell 33
Loubier 34
Louis XIV 9, 10
Luyken, Jan 6

Maillard, Peter 37
de la Marche, Jean 11, 13
Margas 45
Marot, Daniel 43–4, 58
Mary I 9, 28
Marylebone 22
de Mayerne, Théodore 40
Maze 37
medicine 40
Mesman, Daniel 37
Mettayer, Louis 48
Minet 7, 34
Minet and Fector's Bank 34
Monlong, Pierre 43, 46
Museum of London viii, 59

National Maritime Museum 58
Newhouse (or De la Neuvemaison) 50–1
Nogee 23
Norwich 4

Oates, Titus 28
Ogier (or Ougier) 37–8, 59
Old Royal Observatory 58
Olivier 23, 58

opposition to immigrants 27–31, 38–9
Orange Street, French church 58
Ouvry 37

Painting, Academy of 43
Pall Mall 43
Papillon 12, 33
Pelletier, Jean 43, 58
Pepys, Samuel 28
Perreau 32
Peyferié 31
Philip II 3, 28
Piccadilly Circus 58
Pigne, James 37
Pilon, Daniel 37
Pineau, Daniel 37
Plague 10
de Planche, Jean 40, 42
Platel, Pierre 45
poor relief 24, 50, 51, 53–4
Poultrain (or Colt), Maximilien 60
Prangnell, J. 5
Prelleur, Peter 43
printing 40

Ravenel, Abraham 38
Remy 23
Restoration (1660) 11, 13
Revocation of the Edict of Nantes (1685) 8, 19, 29
Riou, Edward 58, 59
Riviete 38
Roberdeau, James 37
Rochester 54
Rocque, John 21
Rondeau, John 37
Roubiliac 60
Rousseau, Jacques 58, 59
Rye 24

Sabatier, John 37

de Sainliens (or Holyband), Claude 40, 43
St Martin Orgars, French church 29
St Paul's Cathedral 40, 59
Savage, Samuel 37
Savary 23, 58
Savoy, French church of the 8, 13–17, 49
Schnebbelie, R. B. 17
schools and schoolmasters 22, 40, 43, 54–5, 57
seamen 22, 32
Seignoret, Etienne 36
Sequeret, Judith 38
Soho district, see Westminster
Soho Square 5, 56–7, 59
soldiers 14, 15
Southampton 24
Spitalfields and the eastern suburbs 14–15, 17–22, 32, 35–8, 43, 53, 59–60
Sunbury-on-Thames 22

Teulon 23, 58

Threadneedle Street, French church 4, 5, 8–15, 24, 57
Tijou, Jean 43, 45, 58, 59
tradesmen 14–15, 17, 28–9

Van Somer 58
le Vautier, Daniel 37
Vautrollier, Thomas 40
Verzelini, Jacob 40–1
Victoria and Albert Museum 60

Walloons 3–4, 33, 35
Wandsworth 22–23, 25, 51
Wapping 22
watchmakers 15, 26, 43, 59
weaving 14–15, 24, 29, 35–8, 59–60
Webb, Aston 56, 59
Westminster and the western suburbs 13, 14–15, 17, 22, 31, 43, 45, 53–59
Westminster Abbey 60
West Street, French church 59
Willaume, David 45
William III 44
Wren, Sir Christopher 16

This postscript, the story of a family's escape to Exeter, provides a vivid description of the difficulties and dangers involved in fleeing France by sea which would have been familiar to many of the Huguenots who ended their lives in late seventeenth-century London.

"I was the eldest of the children of my father and mother, and in their absence was in charge of their household at La Rochelle and of five of my youngest brothers and sisters, of whom the eldest was ten and the youngest, two. I had had my parents' permission to take any chance that might arise to leave the kingdom with all or part of the family.

On 24 April a good friend alerted me that a small boat was leaving for England, and that he had engaged the captain to take four or five people – all he could conceal. The captain would throw a large barrel of wine into the water, and put us in its place in the bilge, on salt. As he risked the loss of everything if he was found out, he wanted a large sum of money, and I promised a thousand French livres, half before embarkation, the other half on arrival at Exeter.

At 8 p.m. on the 27th I took two brothers and two sisters with me, pretending to go for a walk in a place frequented every evening by fashionable society. When the company dispersed at 10 or 11 p.m, we moved in the opposite direction to the road to our house, and headed for the sea wall where we were to enter by a back door where we were awaited. The captain agreed to take my last small sister, my god-daughter, to whom I was especially attached, after I promised she would not cry in the vessel on the two or three occasions it was inspected; I trusted in God's help.

At 2 a.m., four sailors came to the beach at low tide and took us on their shoulders to the boat, me with my small sister in my arms on the head of one. The opening to the hiding-place they had prepared was so tiny, there was a man inside to pull us through. Once we were set in place on the salt, the trap door was closed up again, and nothing could be seen; the place was so low that our heads touched the deck planking above; we took care to hold our heads right under the beams, so that when the inspectors as was their charming custom thrust their swords in, they could not pierce our skulls.

As soon as we were aboard we set sail, and the King's men came to make their inspection. By good fortune we were not discovered, nor on the second and third occasions."

Summarised extract from Suzanne de Robillard's autobiographical account of her family's escape from France, 1687, prepared by the author from *Bulletin de la Société de l'Histoire du Protestantisme Français*, XVII (1868), 487–9.

Printed and bound by CPI Group (UK) Ltd, Croydon, CR0 4YY

14/04/2025

14656918-0001